Some
Words Worth
Reading

BUNNY SILVERLOCK

© Bunny Silverlock 2009
Some Words Worth Reading

ISBN : 978-0-9562045-0-9

Published by William's Books
Beech Hanger
Newham Lane
Steyning
West Sussex
BN44 3LR

"e"mail Colin_Sil@msn.com

Book designed by Michael Walsh at
THE BETTER BOOK COMPANY

and printed by
RPM Print & Design
2-3 Spur Road
Chichester
West Sussex
PO19 8PR

CONTENTS

FOREWORD

Many, many years ago our Granddaughters came and asked my wife if she would contribute to a "Poet Tree" at their School. It was a tree in the School grounds on which they intended to hang poems by the relatives of the children.

The idea caught the imagination of Grandma who produced a "classic" for them embodying all the virtues taught in bygone schooldays. For the first (*and only*) time in his life, Grandpa also joined in with something less virtuous!

Over the next twenty or so years, my dear wife wrote many more, as the mood took her, the majority being funny and zany interspersed with some more serious and profound.

A selection of the best from over the last six years are in this booklet.

C.G.S.
2008

AUTHOR'S PROFILE

Bunny Silverlock

Margaret Annie, known as Bunny since childhood, is now 78 years of age with fifteen grandchildren and nine great-grandchildren. She has been reading bedtime stories to her children and grandchildren for over fifty years.

She has written her own stories, notably the "Miss Pinder" series for their amusement but has to admit that they are too "old fashioned, & innocent" for the majority of young children in today's world.

In addition she is an avid writer of short poems ranging from the serious and profound to downright funny and naughty, initially just for her own amusement.

A country woman with a deep love of children, Bunny has travelled extensively throughout the world, in particular, Europe, Scandinavia, the Middle and Far East and North America accompanying her husband on his business trips. Her interests are reading, gardening, cooking, embroidery, and the South Downs of England where she has lived for the past fifty years.

January 2009

Bunny at her desk

MY THANKS TO IAN TYRRELL –

For the wonderful illustrations throughout this book.

From a very early age Ian has been sketching, as a child on the back of his Father's blueprints of military aircraft which he had brought home from his work and then later at art school followed by a scholarship to art college where he studied graphic design.

In the early 1960s he decided to travel to New Zealand but on the way stopped off at Cape Town to see the sights and decided to stay there which he did for the next 25 years. He never did get to see New Zealand.

Whilst in South Africa he worked for a while on a national newspaper and as art director for an advertising agency, later starting his own successful design studio.

In the 1980s he returned to England with his South African wife and daughter where, with some friends he started an advertising agency in London winning awards for the "best campaign".

They now live in the lovely town of Arundel, West Sussex where he currently works producing illustrations for children's books and other literature. He also exhibits his paintings at the annual Arundel Gallery trail.

Having lived on his own sailing boat for six years in Durban Harbour it is not surprising that boating is his passion. He enjoys painting and drawing marine subjects and has been commissioned to paint a number of pictures of yachts. (www.tyrrellart.com)

Bunny Silverlock

1

When you get to 72

It seems when you get to be seventy-two,
There is always something the matter with you.

Just little things that are hard to bear,
usually covered by underwear.

Nothing serious, nothing grand,
But still very *nasty* you understand.

And if, when asked by friends you meet,
Down at the pub, or in the street,

... friends you meet down at the pub

You simply say that you "are fine"
Giving them not the slightest sign

You've a dreadful itching "under your hat"
you wouldn't wish to bore them with that,

You stoically smile and say "All's well"
because you know it's absolute hell

to have to listen to their complaints,
One would think they were all blessed saints

To put up with symptoms far worse than yours.
Best hurry home and get back indoors

drop down the latch, and have a good scratch,
Just think if you get to be seventy-five

You'll simply be glad that you're still alive!

2

Folklore

The wimmin of Sussex are buxom and brown,
and if love is willing they'll raise up their gown
and lie on the sweet scented turf of the Down.

The sons that they bear are stalwart and true,
with corn coloured hair and eyes of deep blue,
hiding their thoughts from a furriner's view.

… are buxom and bold.

With inborn politeness they listen and nod,
Whilst the black coated clergyman rants about God.
and the vengeance He'll wreak when they're under the sod.

But the wimmin of Sussex are buxom and bold,
in their fat, freckled arms their sons they enfold.
foretelling their future with words yet untold.

"So find thee a maiden, take her up on the Down,
and if love is willing she'll raise up her gown,
'Tis then, my sweet lovely, your heaven is found."

At the top of the Down the sky kisses the land,
Take your young maiden, hold tight to her hand,
There are more things on earth than we understand.

3

3

Old Friends

Old Charlie Peer and Mavis, his wife
Have been wonderful friends of mine
Over the years, the afore-mentioned Peers
Have matured like very fine wine.
Lately we ring and then meet at a Pub –
Preferably choosing one serving good grub,
We talk of the weather, the children, our health
And how Gordon Brown takes our money by stealth.
My darling wife and the fair Mavis Peer,
Gossip in whispers that we cannot hear,
Happy and laughing like little girls,
In their flowery blouses and rows of pearls.
We all know that nobody lives forever
But all the time we can get together
For a bite of lunch and an hours chat
We raise our glasses and drink to that,
Jolly good friends worth their weight in gold
Are one of life's joys now that we have grown old.

Gossip in whispers ...

4

Local Heroes

(Coversation in a public bar c1950 in Dorset.)

"We 'ad quite a to-do 'ere yesterday,
Pity you 'ad to miss it
You chose the wrong Sat'dy to go away
And pay your Auntie a visit,
Seems those young varmints, 'as always bin friends
— lives in them cottages round the last bend
Set out to go fishing just past the weir, —
— Ah thankee kindly, mine is a beer.

Wall, — when they first saw it
They thought t'was a log,
As it came closer they thought t'was a dog,
Then as 'un drew near they saw t'was a mite
Waving 'er arms and crying in fright,
They ran down the bank and into the water,
Up to their arm pits, – they didn't falter,
The biggest one grabbed and hung on to her dress
Whilst her frid'ened young mother, w'cries of distress
Sobbing and running, despr'tly screaming
Bumped into the vicar who was walking by dreaming.
E'd 'eard the cafunkle but thought they was playing,
He shouldn't shut his eyes tight when 'e's a praying!
Big George at the forge, hearing the panic
Shouted at Ted to fetch the mechanic
They ran to the river with ropes and such like
Then P.C. Belchamber rode up on his bike
The amb'lance arrived, bells ringing, lights flashing,
The whole cricket eleven, – my word they looked dashing!

They ran down the bank ...

The 'Ysterical mother, wi er wet little mite
Were driven to Blandford and kept overnight

* * * * *

Ah Landlord, – Two 'alves of bitter when you 'av the time,
Now where 'ad I got to wi   this tale of mine?

* * * * *

By now there was quite a consid'rable crowd
Old Doctor Jeffrey said "We should be proud",
A life had been saved by two of his Scouts
They'd both get their badges wiv out any doubt
I'eard that Malpass the butcher sent up chops for their tea
An' a big bag of toffees from Mrs. McNee

down at the sweet shop; then Colonel Snaithe-Brown
Dug in 'is pocket, give 'em both 'alf a crown,
But then Lady Daph-en-ee up at The Hall
Sent a brown paper parcel, T'was best gift of all
'Er boys 'ad outgrown two 'erring bone jackets
You know the sort, with double back plackets
And 'andsome grey flannels from Saville row
Gentleman's wear, as everyone knows,
Mr. Dobbs, their head teacher, is changing the rule
Says they'll be let to wear them next term at school

If boys of thirteen can be 'ave like grown men
They never need wear their short trousers agen.

5

Ladies Day at the Croquet Club

I girded my loins in virginal white,
left the house at 9.30 to "Fight the good fight"
Arrived at the Clubhouse, found which was my lawn,
Clutching my mallet, – All confidence "gorn"
For there waiting for me, – a formidable femme.
Big bosom, big arms, and a very big B**!

... a formidable femme

Oh! What a morning! – What a defeat!
I spent most of my game "sat out" on the seat.
Watching with envy her consummate skill,
Balls sailed through the hoops, all at her will.
Rushes and take-off's , stop shots _and_ a peel
all done with perfection, such ardour, such zeal.

The afternoon doubles was just as bad,
Jean "G" and I could only look sad.
Watching them pilot, and then pioneer.
four ball and three ball, both in the clear.
Forlorn and defeated we went in for tea,
rushed into the Ladies both needing a P**!
T'was then we discovered once more we'd been beaten,
The best of the cakes had already been eaten.

We said our adieus, "A wonderful day.
so glad we were able to come here and play"
For, being British, we know it's a sin,
Only to play, expecting to win.
But it would have been nice if just one of our group,
had been able to manage at least the first hoop!!

6

"Home Thoughts from Abroad."

But not so nice as Brownings

This year I thought I would travel—not just stay at home,
So; like a sardine packed in a can,— I flew off to see Rome.

* * * * *

The patrone, with a shrug said "We make a mistake-a
Scusi, Signora, your room is a take-a
We do 'ave annozer on ze tentz floor,
rounda da back, – but we charge you no more!!"
The food was expensive, the waiters were rude,
except "Pavarotti" – he was just *LEWD*!!

"... but we charge you no more!!"

Needing a rest I order a coffee
with vanilla ice cream and a slice of banofee,
when I ask "Quanta costa?" he deliberately mumbles
and smirks condescendingly watching my fumbles
to find the right money to pay him exactly
or else he takes all with a swift practised "Grazie"

Jostled by girls, their bosoms escaping
from tight fitting T shirts with neck lines a-gaping;
Their garlic breathed boy friends stomped on my sandals
I swear they descended directly from VANDALS.

Oh – the traffic, the heat, the smells and the dust,
The Churches the Ruins each one a "must";
The taxis, the guide books, the Euros just went –
Exploited, exhausted, utterly spent!
Oh, why did I not just take a big book
out of the library and quietly look
at the Ancient and Modern Splendours of Rome
and spend my time off in the garden at home?

7

Multiple Choice

Preamble :-
A middle aged couple at the breakfast table, he reading the
newspaper whilst she, sitting opposite, talks to him. A way
of communicating to which they were both well adjusted.

"The Hammonds are coming our way next Friday,
I'll ask them to lunch. Oh no! cottage pie day!
Perhaps I'll give Delia a hasty perusal,
Try to find something a little unusual,
What do you think? Chicken chasseure,
or Goujons of Plaice with anchovy-beurre?
Italian lasagne, or Hungarian goulash?
New England chowder, Kentucky hash.
Kidneys Tobago or stuffed loin of pork?
Oh dear, that is sounding like far too much work,
Madras-curried chicken, no that is too hot,
Chilli-con-carne, no I think not,
Ragout of lamb, Sugar glazed gammon,
Just a ham salad or tranches of Salmon?
Perhaps on a Friday they only eat fish,
Then I could try an haute-cuisine dish.
'Coquilles St. Jacques? Portuguese cod?
Served with those peas that are left in the pod.
A Selsey dressed crab. Are they in season?
We cannot have Game for that very same reason,
Simple lamb chops, a Quiche Lorraine,

Somehow they both seem rather mundane,
Boeuf-a-la-croute? that's better at dinner
Polo marengo – now there's a winner
or ....
"Really my dear if you want my advice,
your cottage pie is awfully nice."

I'll give Delia a hasty perusal ...

8

50 years is Half a Century

You took me for lunch at the old Rose and Crown.
Then, in the sunshine we strolled around town
Surprised at how much had stayed just the same,
The quaint river boat-house still had the same name.
The Spinning-Wheel Tea Rooms, the Ritz cinema, where,
after the films we had drinks in the bar.

The passing of time, our memories enhance
Was this ugly brick hall our Palais-de-Danse?
Evocative music – Glen's "String of Pearls"
Handsome young airmen, beautiful girls
All laughing gaily, dispelling their fears
But when a boy crashed – then there were tears.
All of us wishing the war would be over
and Bluebirds would fly again above Dover.

Then you were posted, we both lost touch
Perhaps our "Romance" was not up to much.
You married Annette and raised your two boys
whilst Jack and my girls filled my life with joys.

Time for goodbyes ...

Time for goodbyes, and as I watch you go ...
A DFC holder with hair white as snow
I can still see the daring passionate youth
who, being English, had fought for the Truth.

And I wondered, quite vainly,
what you thought of me
now a fat, dumpy widow of
seventy three!

9

A Nonsense Rhyme

Mr. Zilliarchos and his friend Joe Graziano

Were trekking up a mountain side in the alti-plano

When they met a native fellah dressed in feathers, bones, and hide,

Without a mutual language they just waved their hands "Aside"

His face split in a toothless grin, he smiled from ear to ear,

They were the only white men he had seen so far that year,

Unlike them, he was armed, with cudgel spear and knives,

He thought how well their leather coats
would look upon his wives,

His daughters too would love to have their bags and golden rings,

His sons would like their watches—and other useful things

Mr. Zilliarchos and his friend Joe Graziano

Were never found, deep in a cave, beneath the bats' guano

And the moral of this little tale …

"Do not put unto the test,

The idea that a kindly heart beats in a savage breast."

His face split in a toothless grin ...

10

To Each his Own

They came over for lunch, arriving at noon,
Not one minute adrift, not one minute too soon.
The clock struck the hour as they drove through the gate –
In thirty five years they have never been late!

She stepped out of the car and I gave her a kiss,
She gave me a box: "I know you'll like this,"
I don't need to look they're dark chocolate mints,
"I know their your favorites," – They're not, I like Lintz!

"You've got a new car," says my husband Jack.
He walks round the front and he walks round the back.
"I chose the colour," she says with a laugh,
Why do I think of a coal miner's bath?

"It's called CHEKHOV BLUE, which sounds so romantic,"
"Chekhov was not" — I sound so pedantic
"Not what?" — Romantic, I think —
Lets all go inside – I could do with a drink!

The melon's consumed, Jack's carving the lamb,
When she suddenly asks if we've heard about Pam
Pam is her sister who lives somewhere in Wales,
Either up in the hills or down in the vales.

"Well"— there follows a rigmarole full of dismay
Which lasts through dessert and lunch cleared away,
Jack disappeared along with his brother,
An art they perfected, avoiding their Mother.

After Pam it was Peggy, then Janet, then Joyce,
My whole afternoon drowned out by that voice,
We went into the garden to sit in the sun,
But there's nowhere to hide – nowhere to run,

'Saved by the bell' – when she heard the clock chime
"Oh goodness gracious, can that be the time?
Well goodbye, Mrs Armstrong" – she thinks she's a wit
I say "Goodbye, Mrs Armstrong," and feel such a twit.

In my long happy marriage there has been but one flaw,

My simply impossible Sister-in-Law.

After Pam it was Peggy, then Janet, then Joyce ...

11

The Pre-Christmas Telephone call

(A monologue by an elderly cockney
London mother to her married daughter.)

"She says she's not going to Daphne and Sid,
I thought it was sorted, I honestly did.
'Course when we discussed it way back in June,
We should've known it was was much too soon ...

    to think about Christmas!

Last year when she went to your Aunty Rose.
Things turned very nasty, they both came to blows!
She said the turkey was practically raw
Rose didn't answer, – just quietly swore
but the old lady heard her and gave her a smack,
telling her not to answer her back ...

    a very nice Christmas!

Remember the time with Raymond and Lily
Well, – we all know Ray's Lil is a little bit silly,
She'd forgotten the crackers ... and that
meant no riddles, no mottoes and no paper hats.
She said the pudding was lumpy and stodgy,
It didn't surprise her their girls were so podgy!
Ray brought her home right after "The Queen"
Fed up with her making a bad tempered scene ...

    Oh Happy Christmas!

Remember the time with Raymond and Lily ...

She won't go to Dot, says they make too much noise,
She can't sit down nowhere with all of their toys,
What else d'you expect with two sets of twins
The peace of a Convent where nobody sins?
and Dot was so mingy, – poured only one sherry,
How can that make a person's day merry? ...

Merry Christmas!

Because I'm the eldest they think I can cope,
But every year I still have a hope
That someone will have her and leave Dad and me
to celebrate Christmas around our own tree.
And then I remember when we was all small
How she would manage, with not much at all -
During the war when Dad was away,
fighting the Jerries, She made our day
the best that she could – a difficult task
so I suppose it's not too much to ask,
to sit her down in front of the telly
give her a gin and some strawberry jelly,
Ignore all the grousing and endless grumbling,
The "Burps and the f***t's and the strange tummy rumbling

A "Thank you" for all the good Christmases past,
After all, *this one could well be her last !!*

I love Christmas.

12

The Visitors

A baby has lain on my bed today.
Her nappy was changed and her dress rearranged,
her form is still there in the rose patterned spread,
like a hare's in the field which the tall grasses shield.
She smiled and beguiled with her feminine charms,
then fell fast asleep in her father's strong arms.
Her brother ignored her, eager to feed ...
the pensioned-off ponies, old and knock-kneed
taking the carrots, over the rails, from great-grandpa's
hands,
swishing their tails.

A baby has lain on my bed today.
They left about four and are well on their way,
in the Alpha Romeo, safely to Kele
Robert and Lewi and dear little Ellie,
I hope that the baby who lay on my bed,
waving her fat little arms over her head
catching the sunbeams dancing above her
will always have someone to cherish and love her.

13

Plat du Jour

Fish cakes on Friday! Why am I making them?
Suppressed superstition, (or Alliteration?)
 Why not LAMB chops or a "GOOD SHEPHERD'S pie?
I'm not being facetious – just tell me why …
…. it is fish cakes on Friday – or a fillet of cod
I'm quite sure what I eat does not interest God.

Others are told <u>NO</u> crisp crackling pork
<u>NO</u> breakfast bacon to spear on a fork!
<u>NO</u> gammon and pineapple in a pub garden,
And heaven forbid – <u>NO</u> Casserole lardons
They must not eat this and they must not eat that
And yet quite a lot of them get very fat!

Further afield, I am told they eat dogs!
and nearer home—ze legs of ze frogs!
In China a birds nest is thought velly nice
Everything else comes with mountains of rice.
Aborigine families feast on white maggots,
Out in the Outback they'd hardly find faggots.
Those in the know say "We are what we eat" –
"Poison for one is another man's meat".

Pigs' trotters, Whales' blubber, Bedouin sheeps eyes,
Just think what the Champion Bullfighters prize!
"Enough! Please stop!" I hear you mutter
As I mash the potatoes with a big knob of butter,
Fold in the haddock and they're ready to fry

It's Friday, – it's Fish cakes, but don't ask me why.

14

The expert opinion

Matilda and her sister sat sewing in the shade
Doing their embroidery, when they spied their parlour maid
Approaching them, where they sat, beneath the apple tree.
"Excuse me Mum – the Vicar's come – shall 'e stop for tea?"
"Oh bother," said Matilda, "What a dreadful imposition,
Now our afternoon will be just an inquisition."

* * * * *

"Good afternoon dear Ladies, I prithee and forsooth—"
quoth the vacuous Vicar — (being long in tooth)
Talking with his mouth full and spitting as he spake
His practiced hand reached out to take the biggest slice of
cake.
Without a change in their demeanor, the sisters made a plan,
To rid themselves, once and for all, of this obnoxious man.

* * * * *

"Shall we take a turn about?" asked Matilda, with a smile.
"For Jane and I, in truth, have sat here quite a while."
They wandered through the orchard to a little ruined cott.
Where the poor impoverished peasant folk had tried to work
the plot;
Passing by the dried-up well, Matilda's sister cried,
"Oh dear, kind sir, I'm sure I heard an animal inside,
Do take a look, we'll hold your legs. Not to, would be a sin."

* * * * *

With perfect ease and ne'er a qualm,
the sisters pushed him in!
He did not cry, he did not croak,
for as he fell his neck was broke!
and when they heard the frightful thwack,
they hitched their skirts and hurried back.
"Has't Vicar gone?" their maid enquired,
when she came to take the tray,
"Why yes," Matilda said, "He only came to say
he was off to visit Italy, then Athens' Parthenon,
That will take a year or more, a long time to be gone."

* * * * *

Time has passed, and years rolled by,
    A century or two
And the BBC sent a Dig Deep Team
    (With a camera and crew,)
Bearded, earnest, clever chaps,
who try to find conclusions.
They always tend to say
"Perhaps" to cover their delusions!
But the man in charge who found the bones
said it really wasn't nice,
It looked to him – to all intents –
A human sacrifice.

His practiced hand reached out ...

15

The Honorable Member

There was a man who sought a seat but first was made to stand,
Then he joined that club elite who think they rule the land.
He went into the House and sat on leather covered benches,
Looking very serious — *listing his expenses!*

Looking very serious ...

The West end flat, a pied – a – terre,
For the Whip-line-late night voting,
Absolutely "necessaire"— to keep his daughter doting!
The 90's kitchen so "de trop", he would have to modernise,
And he'd get an HD Plasma screen – *Why economise?*

Frequent flights to Brussels and places further on,
To meet his foreign counterparts in Paris or in Bonn.
To wine and dine in gilded rooms planning "urgent things",
Extending hospitality – "roundabouts and swings"
Lords, Ascot, Henley, Wimbledon,
Just give the nod and it *will be done.*

His wife could type some letters,
make his appointments at the Gym,
Then he could claim her P.A.'s wage just for helping him
His younger son's abilities, not obvious to date:
They could surely find a simple way for him to integrate.
His sister's husband's brother,
now retired from Corporate Banking,
Looking for a Knighthood, *would find some way to thank him.*

Oh such magnamanity when the public foots the bill –
Allowances, expenses, call it what you will.
Take heart dear friend, the day will come
When he will **really** count the cost,
All this profligracy ends *when he finds his seat is lost.*

When this occurs he'll need that friend in Brussels or elsewhere
a commendation from PM, – on his honesty he'll swear
He needs another easy seat where there's general abuse,
his expertise gained in the House could well be put to use
A Secretary, flat and car, expenses never ending,
And **over there** so much *less chance of anyone caught bending.*

16

The Yorkshire Lad

I stand on't scales every Monday
to see if I've lost any weight.
It's hypothetical really, cos
me Mam keeps loading me plate.
"Finish these roasted potatoes,
you know you're a growing lad"
But, – Mam, who is really evil,
does it to upset me Dad.

Me Dad's going on forty
and weighs nearly eighteen stones,
He says it's our Viking Inheritance
gives us these heavy bones.

He says it's our Viking Inheritance ...

He boasts of an earlier ancestor
who once ate a dozen pork pies
But me Mam says the Braithwaite menfolk
have always told fanciful lies!

We go t'football at week-ends
We fully support the game
and on the way there, – and on the way back
me Dad always orders the same,
"A big double Mac wi' plenty of fries
and the same for my lad William John."
Then, wi' a wink, he says to me
"I'll have what you can't manage, son."

He sings Basso Profundo wi' pit head choir,
he makes a beautiful sound,
but me Mam who is evil says it's because
he's so short and so fat and so round
I have a persistent feeling,
I'll confide if you don't think I'm silly
If he gets any larger and cannot bend down
he'll not reach his boot laces – will he?

There's this girl in my class called Susan,
and I'm hoping she'll go on a date
and that is the reason (at my age)
I am so concerned wi' me weight.

Me Mam, being evil as usual
says I haven't remotest chance
As none of the Braithwaite menfolk
have the slightest idea of Romance.

But me Dad's always laughing and joking
He likes being one of the boys
He's first wi' his hand in his pocket
if he hears a man's out of employ.
Up here in our part of Yorkshire
we Braithwaites wi'out any doubt
can prove that there's more than one meaning
for calling an Englishman STOUT.

17

Call to Arms

Mens' arms encircle their women at night
Then, in times of war, carry into the fight
Cudgels and spears, arrows and knives,
Guns and grenades: to end other mens' lives.
Down through the ages the clarion call
excites and invites men into the thrall.
The Glory, the Honour – the CALL to ARMS
Will end in weeping and sorrow, sadness and Psalms.

Men's arms encircle their women at night
They are left sleeping in the dawn's early light.
Men plough, sow and reap —
Husband the animals; Fish in the deep
Mine underground; for Centuries keep
All of their History – down through the ages
In leather-bound books with close written pages.
Painting and Sculpture, Music and Dance
Civilization — given a chance.

Hoisted on shoulders ...

Men's arms still encircle their women at night,
The small laughing child squealing with fright ...
is thrown into the air touching the sky,
Thinking it possible – knows he can fly.
Hoisted on shoulders, o'er heads he can see
Clattering horses, bright pageantry.
Glittering swords catching the sun
Scarlet and Gold : The spell has been spun.
The Glory, the Honour, the CALL to ARMS
All end in weeping and sorrow, sadness and Psalms.

18

The Hospital Visit

" 'Ow are you, Bert, feeling better?
Dot says did you get her letter?
She sends her love, but can't get over,
'er legs are bad and she's still got Rover –
just til Sharon's back in June
and that, she says, can't come too soon!
Gallivanting out in Spain showing people over villas,
more likely showing sights to fellas!

That fair haired girl, works in the shop,
is getting married, to a cop.
and Doreen in the Pig and Whistle
remember 'er, well Bert this'll
show you just how right you were
to warn young Jason not to err
with girls who work behind the bar,

" 'Ow are you, Bert?"

seems she went a bit too far.
The baby's due in September,
Father? says she can't remember!

There's been more fuss with old Fred Strickers –
went in Maud's garden, stole her knickers
'orf 'er clo'es line, – why's 'e do it?
Magistrates will make 'im rue it.
Tho why Maud put's them out on show
is something else that I don't know.
'That new lady at "the Spinney"
says "Ello," she's far too skinny.
every day she looks much thinner
prob'ly doesn't eat 'er dinner
got this "Anoraks" disease,
shouldn't wonder, dursn't sneeze —
She'd surely blow 'erself away!
Not like fat old Phyllis Gray,
she went and joined the W.I.

Thought it was that club to try
to get yer weight down, what a bloomer,
Elsie March was in the room, 'er
said Phyllis sat and looked quite puzzled,
seven cups of tea she guzzled,
saying no to all the cakes,
thinking – well it takes
a firm resolve to make a start
so she just took a treacle tart.

Mrs Dobson's got new curtains
ready mades from Messrs Burtons,
keeps 'em drawn 'alf way acrorst
just in case the point is lorst

on all of us is going past
I just wonder if they'll last

Vicar's 'orf to Spain again
Somewhere with a funny name.
Says 'es sorry 'e can't visit
'e got 'is chance and couldn't miss it
seems 'is friend from boyhood days
'oo knows 'is faults and funny ways
'as booked the crossing in advance,
then they're driving down through France,
sooner them than me, says I
I don't fancy "Frogs-legs-pie"!
Oh well Bert, I'll come next Sunday,
Your brother's coming over Monday.
Anythink you want – just say
Orlright then, I'm on me way
Gord bless you Bert, I must go."

Thanks for coming, goodbye Flo."

19

For the "Poet Tree"

Written for the Grandchildren
for their Poet Tree at school.

By Granny :-

Oh how I love my Country
This England brave and fine.
Her woods, her fields and rivers
And hills that stand in line
    Against a sky of dove-wing grey
    And the rain comes from behind.

Oh how I love my County,
Fair Sussex by the sea.
Her cliffs, her bays, her harbours,
From Rye and Winchelsea
    To Arundel, Chichester and Angmering-on-sea.
    Her hidden, hollow quiet lanes
    That guard her history.

And best I love her Children,
In the playgrounds running free
With soft spoken Sussex voices,
sing praises that they be –
When old enough and wise enough
To know that England's best
And sleepy-silly Sussex ......
will clasp them to her breast.

By Grandpa :-

Oh how I love my Country
It's rain and snow and wind
it never used to be like this
till Heinz put beans in tins.

Oh how I love my County
Fair Sussex by the sea
In every lovely car park,
They let us all "P" free

And best I love her Children,
The nasty little brats,
Putting spiders in their teachers drawers
and tying tins to cats
So lets all cheer our Country
and shout "Hip Hip Hurrah"
Let's also cheer our Grannies,
Not to mention old Grandpa.

20

'Continuum'

"Let's go down and walk by the sea,"
   He said to me.
"Lovely idea, I'll just get my coat,
      After all it's not even three."
Over the Downs, covered with snow,
Walkers and Riders, faces aglow,
Children running, hither and yon gathering snow,
      patting it on,

"Pull down your hat, it's terribly cold"

making a fat little man – who – when
they have gone will melt away, out of sight, into the
night.
(As we fade away when our days are done.)
    Lowest ebb-tide,
Men digging for worms, where the sand firms,
Dogs racing in circles, each freed from his leash.
    Can do as he please,
Joy unconfined, a delight to behold.
"Pull down your hat, it's terribly cold," he said to me.
Taking my hand and making so bold as to kiss me,
    with love in his eyes.
Eyes that were blue, as blue as the skies.
The wintry sun sinking down low,
casting a glorious orange glow —
Whilst far out to sea
great storm clouds were gathered
    all over France,
    I did a dance ...
"It's like William Blake, England is blessed,
Darkened and dammed shall be all the rest."
Not liking the Frogs, smoking their Gauloises
and croaking and choking with haute cuisine —
    if you know what I mean!!
We laughed and we scrambled
over the shingle, back to the car,
    it wasn't far.
In the fast fading light of the short afternoon.
Christmas tree lights in sitting-room windows,
    dispelling the gloom.
Once more indoors, filling the kettle,
lighting the fire, beginning to settle,
    the telephone rang,
"Thomas here, hello Gran,
Jo's had our baby, a beautiful girl,

Mother and Daughter both doing well.
    Her name will be Amy —
Just wait 'til you see her, A lovely pink rose
with a dear little nose, ten fingers and toes"
    — the happiness flowed.

"Here's to Great Grandma" he said to me,
taking my hand as I passed him his tea.

21

The Travellers

"Gallivanting again?" Asked Great-Aunt Jane
"Are you going somewhere sunny ?"
"No" said Tim. – *Aunt Jane loved Tim*
(and would leave him all her money)

"I am going somewhere bleak and cold,
To pan the rivers for nuggets of gold.
I shall need a tent and a union Jack
And I'll be very rich when I get back."

"I think that's the Yukon," said Great Aunt Jane,
"So now it's my turn once again.
In this land it's too hot to wear clothes,
and men can make music using their nose.
They don't build houses, they walk-a-bout ..."
"The Australian Outback" guessed Tim with a shout.

The elderly Aunt and the 8 year old boy –
played this game using every ploy.
Together they spent the afternoon hours,
In her conservatory, burgeoning with flowers.
"That's four to you and three to me,
Now I must get us both some tea."

As between the ferns in the Chinese urns,
With only inches to spare,
She watched Tim manoeuvre with masterly ease
The two big wheels of his chair.

22

When you get to 78

It seems when you get to be Seventy-eight
You have to accept that it's now rather late,
To swim the Channel in record time
Or take poll position at Hockenheim.

Be the fourth man on the great Cresta Run
(Upon my word, that would have been fun!)
To crew a yacht in the Fastnet Race,
Feeling the wind and the waves in your face.

Bowl out the Aussies for a thundering win
Knock up a Century when your side goes IN.
Jump four clear rounds at the Hickstead course,
Mounted on an incredible horse.

Shoot white water rapids in a dug out canoe,
So many things that you just did not do!
Out in New Zealand go bungee-jumping.
Abseil down cliffs, hear your heart thumping.
Hang-glide from the Dyke like a bird in the sky.
So many things that you just did not try!

* * * * *

The shower takes an hour and you must not fall over,
Forget about swimming to Calais from Dover!

In Formula 1 before the first lap,
You'd need to lie down and take a short nap!

Abseil down cliffs …

As for the bobsleigh that needs great skill,
Even the Ferry boat makes you quite ill!

You haven't played cricket since you were at school,
Up on a horse you feel such a fool!

White water rapids would terrify you,
Come to your senses and find things to do,

Like walking the dog – when the weather is fine,
If you don't overdo it – you'll reach Seventy-nine.

THE END